Patagonia

Warwick Publishing
Toronto Los Angeles
www.warwickgp.com

Patagonia

ISBN 1-894020-65-0

Warwick Publishing Inc.
162 John Street
Toronto, Ontario, Canada M5R 2E5

Warwick Publishing
Toronto   Los Angeles
www.warwickgp.com

Printed and bound in Brazil

Publishers
Manrique Zago
León Goldstein

Text
Axel Bos

Photographs
Axel Bos, Daniel Rivademar

Editor
Mariana Vicat

Design and Layout
Javier Cedrés

Contents

1 - Introduction
General Aspects of Patagonia — Natural Resources — Climate — Brief Historical Background

2 - The Patagonian Seacoast
Types of Coasts — Geographical Anomalies and Landmarks — Biological Diversity — Natural Resources —
Human Activities — Tourism

3 - The Patagonian Steppe
The Desert-like South — The Plateaus — The Great Rivers — The Petrified Forests — The Estancias

4 - The Forests and the Southern Andes
The Planet's Southernmost Forests — Biological Diversity — Lakes and Rivers — The Great Mountains —
The Patagonian Continental Ice Fields and Glaciers — The Southern Archipelagos

5 - Tourism in Patagonia
Tourist Zones — Principal Attractions of Argentine Patagonia:
The Eastern Zone, the Western Zone, the Southern Zone —
Principal Attractions of Chilean Patagonia: Regions XII, XI, X and IX

Introduction

If we look at a globe, we see that Patagonia is the planet's southernmost region. It makes up the narrowest part of the South American triangle, culminating in a great archipelago with numerous islands of varied size, just 700 miles (1,100 kilometres) from the Antarctic Peninsula. For a long time now, the name Patagonia has evoked images of enormous expanses of land, of seashores that seem to have sprung from the imagination of Jules Verne, and of mountains and glaciers that form one of the world's most extraordinary geological phenomena, all enveloped in a shroud of solitude and mystery that seduces and delights its scarce settlers as well as travelers and explorers. Patagonia is one of the last spots on earth where nature can still be experienced and observed just as it was at the beginning of time, in all its energy and infinite variety. From an ecological point of view, Patagonia boasts a unique natural wealth, including various botanical and zoological species that exist only in this region of the planet. The region is composed of three natural environments: the coastal regions, the steppe, and the southern forests in the Patagonian Andes. The diverse landscapes of these environments are inhabited by flora and fauna that have adapted to their harsh climates of scarce rainfall (except in the western region), virtually relentless and blustering winds, sweltering summers (especially in the northern half), and cruel winters, with heavy snowfall in the southern half (where blizzards have caused serious problems for the rural population). Patagonia was once home to various aboriginal peoples who arrived with the great migratory drift from North America, which in turn was made up of the descendants of those who had arrived from Asia via the Bering Strait.

These hunting, fishing and gathering cultures adapted their ways of life easily to the harsh conditions of the region — until the arrival of the white man. It was at Puerto San Julián in Santa Cruz in 1520 that Portuguese explorer Ferdinand Magellan disembarked during his expedition to seek a passage through South America from the Atlantic to the Pacific. Thus began Patagonia's age of European exploration, stimulated by economic, colonizing and scientific interests. This vast territory was discovered little by little; for many it brought disillusionment; for some it proved to be a challenge; and for yet others, it simply inspired awe. Today, for those who appreciate the natural world, Patagonia is one of the world's most alluring places. It is unparalleled for enjoying the mysteries of the unknown, for exploring the kind of landscapes thought to have been lost forever, and for discovering nature's magnificent ability to surpass all dreams.

The Patagonian Seacoast

The city of Puerto Deseado, strategically located on the Argentine Sea, is an important fishing center. It has also become a popular destination for ecological tourism. Besides the richness of the river's fauna, the area offers easy access, both to the north and to the south, to sites with abundant populations of coastal birds and mammals.

The largest of the estuaries are the outlet of the Santa Cruz River, followed by the estuary of the Gallegos River (where the capital of the province of Santa Cruz is found), and then that of the Coig River.

The most conspicuous geographical feature of the Patagonian coast is the Valdés Peninsula in Chubut. Quite rich in its topographical variety, the peninsula's unusual shape has given rise to two large, somewhat closed-in gulfs: the San José Gulf to the north, and the Nuevo Gulf to the south.

The Nuevo Gulf is the larger of the two. Situated on its west coast is the city of Puerto Madryn, a hub of the tourism industry in the northeast of the province. Visitors flock here to observe the Valdés Peninsula's vast biological riches. A provincial wildlife reserve, it protects a remarkable range of fauna: southern right whales, southern elephant seals, southern sea lions, killer whales, various sea bird species, and an intriguing range of land animals.

On the smaller San José Gulf, highly skilled shellfish divers practice their time-honored craft, harvesting mainly vieyra and cholga, two regional mollusks. Shellfish diving is a discipline that demands great physical strength and fortitude. The divers have to spend hours on end submerged in the icy cold waters of winter, and live for weeks or months in precarious coastal shelters far from the comforts of home.

From an ecological point of view, the coastal lands represent one of

Patagonia's most outstanding regions, inhabited by a rich and diverse range of species. To the already mentioned areas, dozens more could be added, from Río Negro southwards, where breeding colonies for thousands and thousands of specimens exist. Eighteen species of coastal birds and two species of sea lions, as well as some crustacean species, breed in the coastal waters. In addition, Patagonia has the only breeding colony of southern elephant seals on the South American continent.

Many of these places are legally protected by official conservation plans. As well as their intrinsic worth, they represent valuable tourism resources. Each year a growing number of travelers are drawn to the region in search of nature in its pristine state.

The enormous concentration of animal life on the Patagonian coast arises from the great nutritional wealth provided by the South Atlantic. The cold ocean waters are the ideal environment for the proliferation of phytoplankton, the tiny algae that make up the base of the ocean's food chain. The phytoplankton are consumed by animal plankton, particularly by krill, a small prawn rich in protein. Almost all marine species, directly or indirectly, feed on krill, and the population density of coastal birds and mammals depends on their abundance.

Humans also make use of marine resources, although, regrettably, usually without the care necessary to ensure their preservation. Overfishing and non-selective catching methods that senselessly eliminate unprofitable species are resulting in a progressive decline in fish populations, upsetting the ocean's complex and delicate balance. One consequence of this rapaciousness is the deterioration of a food industry that is essential to human survival.

Facing the cliffs of the Valdés Peninsula, in Chubut.

Puerto Pirámide and its surroundings on the Valdés Peninsula.

The cove at Monte León, Santa Cruz *(following page)*.

The varied landscape of the Patagonian coast evokes the thrill of discovery for visitors; its pristine natural environment attracts both scientific and tourist interest.

The cliffs that run down the coast are like great watchtowers overlooking the majestic countryside and sea.
The successive capes, points, bays and coves that make up the coastline inspire an urge to go exploring *(opposite page)*.

Points, beaches and cliffs in the Monte León area of Santa Cruz. This coastal region is one of the most outstanding due to its awe-inspiring scenery, which alternates massive rock formations with long, flat stretches of sand and gorse. It is also an important breeding sanctuary for marine fauna.

The turquoise waters of the Patagonian sea contrast with the faded steppe, creating an inspiring sight for travelers coming from the lands of the interior. When the sea is calm, the shoals — the compacted sands of ancient sea beds — become clearly visible. Like submerged islands, they serve as refuges for the fish, crustaceans and mollusks that inhabit these frigid waters. In summer, the water warms up to 68°F (20°C), whereas in winter its temperature remains stable at 50°F (10°C). The low temperatures cause essential nutrients to rise from the ocean floor. The density of these nutrients increases as the water temperature drops, which explains why the southern seas are among the richest in nutritional wealth.

Following the emergence of the Andes mountain range, this area experienced great volcanic activity. This produced the outcrops of igneous rock seen along the Patagonian coast. Contrasting strongly with the sandstone cliffs, these areas provide excellent sites for the establishment of bird and animal colonies.

The rocky cliffs of Cape Blanco, the highest of their type on the Patagonian coast, extend out into the sea. A lonely lighthouse dominates this natural area, which has been declared a protected reserve due to its unique population of southern fur seals and marine birds.

Penguin Island, south of Puerto Deseado, Santa Cruz *(opposite page)*.

The Penguin Island lighthouse dominates the spectacular coastal area to the south of Puerto Deseado, across from the Oso Marino Bay and the elongated Isla Chata, which harbors Patagonia's largest imperial shag breeding colony, with more than ten thousand nests.

In some places along the Patagonian coast, the wide-ranging tides allow access on foot to sites that otherwise would be inaccessible. In Santa Cruz there can be as much as a 45-foot (14-metre) drop in the water level between high tide and low tide. The tides rise and fall at alarming rates, representing a serious danger for unwary visitors; in some places, rising waters can trap them in the cliff-lined bays and coves. The great caverns of the Monte León area are a perfect example of this; they can only be visited during low tide, when they offer spectacular sights, difficult for even the best of photographers to capture *(following pages)*.

The small village of Puerto Pirámide *(above left)* is the only settlement on the Valdés Peninsula. Nestled in a deep bay off the Nuevo Gulf, it is picturesque and peaceful, surrounded by beautiful natural scenery. Some homes dating from the first decades of this century, when around a thousand inhabitants lived here, have been preserved. The area has become the most popular vacation spot in northeast Chubut due to the Valdés Peninsula's natural attractions.

The Punta Pirámide Wildlife Reserve *(above)*, near the village of the same name, was created to protect an important South American sea lion rookery as well as the abundant deposits of fossils found in this area. Its cliffs are excellent vantage points for observing the southern right whales that make their home in the coastal waters during winter and spring.

The small port in the city of Rawson, the capital of the province of Chubut, is located on the outlet of the Chubut River. Its activities revolve around the small fishing boats that head out to the open seas each day to cast their nets.

During the South Atlantic's summer, southern right whales remain in the sub-Antarctic seas where they feed voraciously and build up the blubber reserves they need to face the rest of the year without eating. Following autumn, they begin their northern migration, arriving in May in the waters of the Valdés Peninsula's Nuevo and San José Gulfs (in Chubut), where they stay until December. These sheltered, tranquil gulfs are the ideal environment for the female whales to give birth and to mate, either for the first time or after weaning their last offspring. These mild-mannered and gentle marine mammals frequently swim very close to the shore, offering visitors to these coastal areas excellent opportunities to observe their behavior, especially in the areas of Puerto Pirámide and Punta Pardela on the Nuevo Gulf. More direct contact can be made on whale-watching vessels that bring tourists within a few yards of the enormous bodies of these 35-ton creatures, affording the chance to observe the interaction between mother whales and their young, the games and mating rituals of adult whales, and above all, the great leaps out of the water by adults and young alike. For a long time now these cetaceans have been studied by marine biologists on the Valdés Peninsula. It has been determined that their population is growing, which is very good news considering their numbers were once dwindling due to extensive whale hunting.

The tail of the adult southern right whale reaches up to 16.5 ft. (5 m) in length. The whale frequently spends up to several minutes in a vertical position with its tail out of the water.

The adult South American sea lion male *(above)* is easily distinguished from the female by its much greater size and by its enormous neck and head which are covered with a mane.

There are numerous South American sea lion rookeries along the Patagonian coast *(left)*. During the summer the sea lions gather in the breeding grounds to give birth and mate, forming harems of several females for each male. The rest of the year they disperse and roam around different coastal areas.The most noteworthy rookeries are those of the Valdés Peninsula in Chubut and that of Monte Loayza in Santa Cruz.

The coasts of the Valdés Peninsula in Chubut are the southern elephant seals' only continental breeding grounds. They are the world's largest seal species, males reaching 20 feet (6.5 m) in length, and females, 10 feet (3.25 m). In July, the bulls return from the sea and establish their territories; later, the females arrive to form their harems, give birth, and then mate again *(above)*.

During this period, visitors can observe the activities of these animals on the beach, such as the fierce fights between bulls defending their harems and territory, and the females nursing their pups. The best place for this is the Punta Cantor Wildlife Reserve, where a great number of elephant seals gather each year. This site is extremely accessible — visitors can walk up and observe the seals from just a few yards away *(upper right)*.

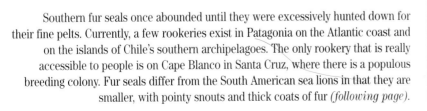

Southern fur seals once abounded until they were excessively hunted down for their fine pelts. Currently, a few rookeries exist in Patagonia on the Atlantic coast and on the islands of Chile's southern archipelagoes. The only rookery that is really accessible to people is on Cape Blanco in Santa Cruz, where there is a populous breeding colony. Fur seals differ from the South American sea lions in that they are smaller, with pointy snouts and thick coats of fur *(following page)*.

The commerson's dolphin (black and white dolphin) is one of the most colorful species of dolphin in the world. It inhabits the Patagonian sea and the Tierra del Fuego region. They can be seen cruising the estuary of the Deseado, the ports of San Julián and Santa Cruz in the province of Santa Cruz (Argentina), and the Strait of Magellan (Chile). They usually swim in groups around the boats. Although they are easy to observe due to their coastal habits, little is known about their biology and population. Studies should be done, as these magnificent creatures do face threats — they are used as bait in traps for spider crabs and get trapped in fishing nets. Legal measures should be taken to prevent these risks, and protected reserves need to be established in the areas the commerson's dolphin frequents.

Two orcas traverse Caleta Valdés on the coast of the Valdés Peninsula, Chubut, looking for prey. These magnificent cetaceans feed on a great variety of species; they are known for their ability to catch elephant seals and sea lions both in the water and even at the edge of stony beaches where they run part of their bodies aground in order to catch any unsuspecting animals that may be lying there.

The great nutritional wealth of the Patagonian Sea has resulted in the proliferation of enormous quantities of sea birds that reproduce in numerous places along its shores. During the southern spring, diverse species flock to nesting colonies to breed. Kelp gulls are the most common birds along the coast. The principal predatory species, they feed on eggs and young snatched from the nests of other sea birds. A kelp gull colony on the estuary of the Deseado River.

While Magellanic oyster catchers nest on the lagoons of the foothills in Santa Cruz, they flock in great numbers to the seashore, moving from beach to beach.

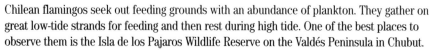

Chilean flamingos seek out feeding grounds with an abundance of plankton. They gather on great low-tide strands for feeding and then rest during high tide. One of the best places to observe them is the Isla de los Pajaros Wildlife Reserve on the Valdés Peninsula in Chubut.

Rock cormorants *(above)* and imperial shags *(page 48)* are the most abundant of the five cormorant species in Patagonia. The former form breeding colonies of various sizes, always on flat land and often with several thousand nests; the latter establish their colonies principally on the edges of cliffs and, on rare occasions, on flat land near the imperial shags *(opposite page)*.

Isla de los Pajaros, an island located in the San José Gulf off the Valdés Peninsula, is one of the best known bird sanctuaries on the Patagonian coast. It is the nesting site of various species, such as seagulls, cormorants, ducks, oyster catchers, and herons. A land bridge between the mainland and the island emerges twice daily at low tide. Nevertheless, visitors are prohibited so as not to disturb the bird population.

One of the wildlife rarities of the Patagonian Atlantic is the red-legged cormorant, which is found exclusively on the coast of Santa Cruz. Its presence there is somewhat puzzling; since this species usually inhabits the western coast of South America, it is unknown how this isolated population came to be. Its principal colonies are found on Cabo Guardian and the estuary of the Deseado River, in Santa Cruz.

One very colorful coastal bird is the dolphin gull, which nests in small groups near other bird colonies. The population on Punta Tombo in Chubut has been the object of scientific study, as shown by the tag on the specimen pictured above.

Magellanic penguins come ashore at the same places to gather in the same nests with the same mates as years before to breed and hatch their eggs. The males begin to arrive at the end of August to get their nests ready to receive the females in September.

After mating and laying their eggs, both males and females share the responsibilities of incubation for 40 days, after which their young hatch. Between February and March, the young are the first to take off for their almost yearlong stay at sea. The adults finally abandon their colonies in April to take to the sea, traveling as far as the latitudes of Brazil.

The largest colony of Magllanic penguins is on Punta Tombo in Chubut with a population of approximately 500,000 adults; however, there has been a considerable reduction in their numbers since the mid-1990s.

On Penguin Island, south of Puerto Deseado in Santa Cruz, a small rockhopper penguin colony was discovered in the 1980s.
It is the only known breeding colony of this species in the Patagonian Atlantic.

The estuary of the Deseado River is a 25-mile (40-km)-long inlet through which the Deseado River, heading from the west of the province, empties into the sea.
Its waters are subject to the local tides, which produce strong incoming and outgoing currents. The estuary is predominantly rocky,
with several islands in its interior where sea bird and sea lion colonies have settled. This area is an outstanding animal life sanctuary. On its
northeast coast sits the city of Puerto Deseado, which has some of the busiest maritime traffic on the Patagonian sea *(opposite page)*.

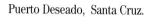
Puerto Deseado, Santa Cruz.

The Marjorie Glen is a ship that caught fire on the Gallegos River in 1912, running aground on Point Loyola. The coast of Patagonia is a great cemetery of ships wrecked over the years, particularly along the coasts of Tierra del Fuego and its adjacent islands.

The railroad line running through northern Santa Cruz was created to link the rural towns of the provincial interior with Puerto Deseado. It provided a much-needed export route for the wool produced on the *estancias* (sheep ranches) in the area and an import route for supplies, which arrived by boat from Buenos Aires. Puerto Deseado's train station is Patagonia's greatest architectural attraction.

The sprawling beach on Cabo Vírgenes, as seen from its lighthouse, is one of the most inspiring views of the Patagonian coast. On clear days, one can see as far as the Strait of Magellan and the northern coast of Tierra del Fuego's Isla Grande. This is the southernmost extreme of Argentina's continental Patagonia, as well as the site of the world's third largest Magellanic penguin colony, with approximately 180,000 specimens registered. This zone has become especially vulnerable due to the petroleum industry activities being developed there over the past decade. For this reason strict regulations are needed in order to eliminate pollution risks to the natural environment and its fauna. This place is also known for the gold dust existing on its beaches, which has always attracted fortune hunters. The most famous of them, Conrado Asselborn, lived in solitude for decades in the house that can be seen at the foot of the cliff, until he committed suicide in 1992 *(following spread)*.

The Patagonian Steppe

The steppe makes up the majority of Patagonia. It extends from the south of Mendoza down to approximately the 51 degree southern latitude in Santa Cruz, and from the southern forests over to the coast (in the north and northeast it is irregularly present).

Its landscapes are characterized by successions of plateaus, many of volcanic origin, alternating with undulating plains. These descend like a staircase eastwards along the arid terrain, which is covered with shrub-like vegetation adapted to scarce rainfall and mighty winds.

Some of the rivers that empty into the sea wind through the plains. They have created beautiful valleys that contrast with the steppe's general monotony. In some of these valleys various agricultural activities have developed to great success, such as fruit- and vegetable-growing. The Río Negro Valley in northern Patagonia has become a major agricultural center.

The Colorado River, which originates in Neuquén and empties into the sea south of Buenos Aires, is the region's longest river, and marks its northern frontier. Two other great waterways cross the southern semi-desert lands: The Chubut River is a vital resource for the generation of hydroelectric energy in the northeast of Chubut. The Santa Cruz River serves as the outlet to the Atlantic for Lakes Argentino and Viedma, both located in the southwest of the province. These lakes are fed by the eastern slope of the Patagonian Continental Ice Field, and extend dozens of miles into the steppe.

There are four lakes on the southern steppe: Lake Musters and Lake Colhue Huapí in the central south of Chubut, and Lake Strobel and Lake Cardiel in the central west of Santa Cruz. These bodies of water occupy depressions produced by the sinking of the earth's crust. Some of these depressions have remained dry, the deepest being the Great Hollow of San Julián in the central east of Santa Cruz, 345 feet (105 m) below sea level.

Patagonia's seemingly inexhaustible paleontologic riches have always attracted the interest of scientists, and the most spectacular discoveries have been made on the steppe. Year after year, great quantities of fossils are unearthed. The fossilized remains of various species of dinosaurs, mammals and other animal groups now enhance the collections of the region's excellent museums. There are also important areas

The Patagonian steppe around Punta Pirámide, Nuevo Gulf, Chubut

Beside the road to the desert, a calden tree adorns the landlocked twilight. The province of La Pampa is the gateway to the Patagonian region north of the Río Negro. Its natural environment of solitary expanses offers the traveler a hint of the great desolate territories that await south of the Colorado River *(previous page).*

both in Chubut and Santa Cruz containing gigantic tree fossils, the forebears of the araucaria tree. The most outstanding sites are the José Ormachea Provincial Reserve in the central south of Chubut, and the Petrified Forest Natural Monument in the northwest of Santa Cruz. Both locations feature enormous petrified trunks of wood in striking colors strewn over the ground. They are what remains of arboreal species that once stood as high as 300 feet (100 m).

Aside from having shaped the typical steppe vegetation, the rigorous climatic and environmental conditions have influenced the evolution of animals with unusual biological features, including some species found exclusively in the region. Typical inhabitants include the guanaco, the Patagonian hare, the small gray fox, and the choique, also known as the petiso (the American ostrich). Many others are less easily observed, but they make up a unique animal population that has warranted extensive scientific study.

Beginning in the mid-nineteenth century, the steppe's great territorial expanses inspired colonization efforts. Over the years, livestock operations, called *estancias,* emerged. Most are dedicated to the breeding of sheep, which graze on the nutritious grasses of the arid south.

The estancias vary in size, the largest being in Santa Cruz and Tierra del Fuego. The typical estancia comprises the proprietor's house, the workers' dwellings, a large woolshed for shearing, and other related structures, all grouped together in one spot. In other spots throughout the estancia there are *puestos,* which generally consist of one lone house that is home to a resident shepherd charged with tending the sheep in that sector.

Over the last decades, the sheep-breeding industry has faced financial difficulties. Consequently, there is now a growing trend to convert these estancias into tourist sites. Many offer visitors the attraction of lodging in centuries-old rural mansions and the opportunity to visit sites of great natural and archaeological wealth. Some of these converted estancias also offer convenient access to national parks and wildlife reserves.

The steppe, under the reign of wind, solitude and silence, is a pristine land brimming with mystery, capable of transporting us back to a forgotten time when there were no maps and few humans had ever set foot on the Patagonian landscape.

The plateaus of the Patagonian steppe descend from the west like a staircase, culminating in the cliffs and lowlands of the Atlantic coast. Its vegetation stretches to the border of the beaches, making for a striking contrast in landscapes between the austere steppe and the intense blues of the sea *(left page).*

Gravel roads crisscross the steppe linking towns and estancias and stretching out towards the endless horizons of the vast and desolate south *(above).*

The quilembai is one of the most famous plant species of the Patagonian steppe, covering great tracts of land with its yellow hues. In the middle distance, the edge of a plain can be made out, with its different geological layers and the typical furrows produced by the erosion of rainwater.

The harsh climate, scarce rainfall and practically nonstop blustering winds of the Patagonian steppe have caused plant species to evolve in compact and shrubby shapes. Their tough leaves have little surface space so that evaporation from exposure to the sun and the pounding of the dry winds is kept to a minimum.

The valleys formed by the rivers flowing eastward are often of exceptional beauty. Such is the case with the Valle de los Altares, in the province of Chubut, through which the Chubut River runs. These valleys, protected from the fiercest steppe winds, have always been the preferred places for human settlement, as the rivers provide the water necessary for agriculture. These settlements are easily recognizable from a distance by the towering groves that surround their dwellings and related structures.

On the coastal steppe, the moderate temperatures produced by the sea, as well as its humid breezes, have created better conditions for the development of vegetation than those on the inland steppe *(following page)*, where species are even more compact in order to withstand the severe climate.

The Chubut River begins its course in the northwest of the province of Chubut and crosses its width to empty into the Argentine Sea. It winds through beautiful valleys and regions like the Iglesias Ravine, in the area beyond the Florentino Ameghino Dam, with its stunning scenery of enormous rocky cliffs.

The lunar landscape of the José Ormachea Provincial Geological Reserve in Chubut *(above right)*, with its stratified formations composed of sediments and volcanic ash.

The petrified forests offer the ultimate example of Patagonian aridity and desolation. Immersed in their eerie stillness, travelers feel transported to another time.

In the province of Santa Cruz, the Petrified Forest Natural Monument conserves impressive examples of ancient araucarias.

One hundred and fifty million years ago, the Patagonian environment was very different from what it is today. At that time, it had a temperate climate that encouraged the growth of great forests. As the Andes did not then exist, the humid Pacific winds crossed the entire region, resulting in abundant rainfall. With the intense volcanic activity that buried vast expanses of territory under ash, the process of fossilization began. Great coniferous species predominate in the Patagonian petrified forests; however, remains have also been found of other botanical groups, such as mushrooms and ferns.

The great stretches of yellow broom sedge in the areas that receive the greatest rainfall add a note of color to the steppe, contrasting with the dark greens of the pepper tree and other shrubby growths. This grass-like species, which is the principal source of nourishment for the region's sheep, tends to stand more than two feet in height. The wind shakes and jolts these plants, producing one of the most characteristic sounds on the Patagonian steppe.

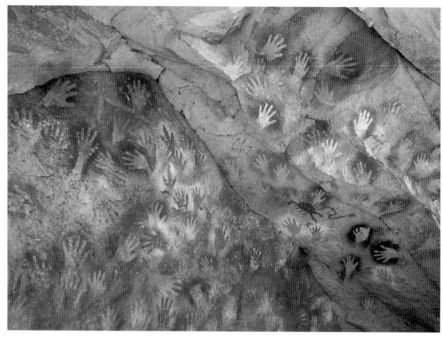

In many places, the steppe is furrowed with gorges and ravines *(above left)* of various shapes and sizes through which, in times of heavy rainfall, run small rivers and streams that quickly disappear. Many of these ravines are formed by great rocky cliffs that sometimes contain hollows of various sizes. In times past, these hollows served as refuges for the region's aboriginal peoples, as evidenced by the archaeological treasures of the Cave de las Manos *(above)*, in the Pinturas River Ravine *(left)*, in the province of Santa Cruz, as well as many other, lesser-known places. Equally priceless are the cave systems with spectacular examples of prehistoric art, such as Estancia La Maria near the coastal city of Puerto San Julián; the caves along the Shehuen River, on the way to Lake San Martin; and the Gualicho Caves on the outskirts of El Calafate.

Rocky ravines near the Chubut River in the Piedra Parada region in the northwest of the province.

In the foothill zones of the steppe, it is common to see lagoons with transparent waters and fairly abundant vegetation along their shores. These lagoons are feeding and breeding sites for various bird species.

Broom sedge-covered steppe in the area of Lake Argentino in southwestern Santa Cruz. This lake extends several miles into the steppe, surrounded by some of the most desolate landscapes of Patagonia *(following page)*.

The powerful Santa Cruz River, an important hydroelectric resource, carries the waters of Lakes Argentino and Viedma to the Atlantic Ocean.
In 1877, the famous geographer and explorer Francisco P. Moreno, accompanied by Carlos M. Moyano, made an extraordinary expedition up this river and gave Lake Argentino its name.

Narrow backroads lead to the agricultural and livestock establishments that abound in the Patagonian steppe. In the mid-19th century, the presence of the white man in Patagonia began to become permanent with the establishment of the sheep-raising estancias. Occupation of all the southern territory was complete by the 1920s. During the following decades, these estancias produced an economic boom, but an inadequate system of production management led to an overpopulation of sheep, which in turn led to overgrazing, resulting in the dreaded desertification of the land. A drop in international wool prices also had a profound impact on the industry. As a result, the number of estancias in the region has declined; for example, of the 1,200 establishments that once existed in the province of Santa Cruz, only 600 are still operating. In recent years, some proprietors, taking advantage of the boom in nature tourism, have converted part of their estancias into elegant and inviting lodgings for travelers, conserving their own attractive style of rural life and offering alternatives for enjoying the rich nature that surrounds them.

Once a year the sheep are gathered in the woolsheds of the estancias to be sheared. For several days, this activity is intense, the shearers undertaking their arduous work for hours on end. In the past, shearing was done with scissors, which required much more labor time than today's modern electric shearers. These skilled men belong to shearing guilds and are contracted specifically to perform this work.

The La Trochita railroad *(following spread)* is outfitted for one of the few trains with a 30-inch (75-cm) gauge still operating in the world. Its original course linked the town of Ingeniero Jacobacci in Río Negro with the city of Esquel in Chubut. Currently, however, it is only active along the Chubut stretch between Esquel and the town of El Maiten. This old train, with its picturesque wooden cars and steam engine, is used by locals and country people to move back and forth between stations. It is also a tourist attraction enjoyed by numerous Argentine and foreign travelers.

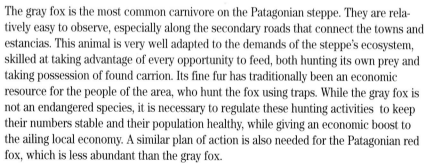

The gray fox is the most common carnivore on the Patagonian steppe. They are relatively easy to observe, especially along the secondary roads that connect the towns and estancias. This animal is very well adapted to the demands of the steppe's ecosystem, skilled at taking advantage of every opportunity to feed, both hunting its own prey and taking possession of found carrion. Its fine fur has traditionally been an economic resource for the people of the area, who hunt the fox using traps. While the gray fox is not an endangered species, it is necessary to regulate these hunting activities to keep their numbers stable and their population healthy, while giving an economic boost to the ailing local economy. A similar plan of action is also needed for the Patagonian red fox, which is less abundant than the gray fox.

The guanaco has adapted superbly to the steppe — its thick wool protects it from the cold and the wind, its feeding habits do not deplete the vegetation, and its hooves do not damage the steppe's grasses. Contrast this with the domesticated sheep which have gravely damaged the vegetation and soil of the Patagonian steppe. The guanaco lives in groups of varying size, the most legendary being the great herds of hundreds of guanacos recorded by Francisco P. Moreno during his expeditions. In the 20th century, guanaco hunting intensified, reducing its numbers. Before this, it had only been hunted by the aboriginal peoples, who ate its meat and used its pelt for clothing, without seriously affecting its population. Nevertheless, guanacos continue to thrive and they are frequently seen in the areas off the main roads, particularly in the many protected areas of the region, such as the Valdés Peninsula and Cabo Dos Bahías in Chubut (Argentina), and Torres del Paine National Park in Magallanes (Chile).

The *choique* or *ñandu petiso* (the lesser rhea, otherwise known as the American ostrich) was once a food source for the aboriginal population, and it has been traditionally hunted by rural settlers for its exquisite meat. It is the largest Patagonian bird and has interesting habits. For example, reproductive tasks are carried out by the male; several females lay their eggs in the same nest and the males incubate them and later take control of caring for and raising the chicks.

The Forests and the
Southern Andes

The Aluminé River draws off water from the large lakes in the southwest of the province of Neuquén. Along its course, numerous minor rivers born of these lakes unite with the Aluminé, increasing its volume and flow. After its juncture with the Chimehuín River, it is called the Collón Curá, which in turn joins with the Limay River, which stems off Lake Nahuel Huapí, the well-known body of water shared by Neuquén and Río Negro. The Limay's energy-producing potential has been put to good use through great works of engineering like the Piedra de Aguila Dam, the Alicurá Dam, and the El Chocón Hydroelectric Dam, constructed in the 1970s. Passing the dams, heading northeast, the Limay joins with the Neuquén River to form the Río Negro, which finally empties into the Argentine Sea.

From Neuquén on southwards, the Andes begin to drop in altitude, allowing the humid South Pacific winds to cross over to the east. This climatic factor provides the rainfall that has led to the planet's southernmost forests and the creation of Patagonia's most beautiful region.

The Patagonian-Andean forest stretches from the central west of Neuquén to Isla de los Estados in Tierra del Fuego. In marked contrast with the arid steppe to the east, it is adorned by a great variety of vegetation that alternates from north to south on both sides of the Andes along a strip a few dozen miles wide.

Among its most outstanding botanical species are the monkey puzzle tree (unique to Neuquén), the larch, the coehue, the Andean cypress, the southern beech, the Antarctic beech, the hard oak, and the evergreen beech. Sour cherry trees and cinnamon trees make up the evergreen forests on the southeast of Isla Grande (Tierra del Fuego) and on Isla de los Estados.

Other minor species grow, protected by the towering trees. The Valdivian forest, which is predominantly on the western side of the Andes, has the most humid climate; its vegetation brings the tropics to mind, with dense thickets of *coligüe* (a grass-like leafy creeper) and epiphytic varieties that grow in the areas of greatest annual rainfall.

Many birds and animals inhabit the area. The most common are the Andean deer (inhabiting a few remote areas), the miniature deer (well adapted to the Valdivian forest), the Magellanic woodpecker, and the condor, the great symbol of the Andes. The puma also deserves special mention, as it is the largest predator of the region, although it can be found in the steppe as well.

The Ice Age left behind spectacular lakes surrounded by mountains in the Patagonian west, which enthrall the traveler with their dream-like vistas. The majority are found in Neuquén and Chubut, where Nahuel Huapí and Los Alerces National Parks are favorite tourist attractions.

The largest lakes, many of which stretch out into the Patagonian steppe, are found in Santa Cruz — Lake Buenos Aires, which on the Chilean side is called General Carreras Lake; Lake Argentino, with its river branches Rico and Sur; and Lake Viedma. The latter two form a great basin and are connected by the La Leona River, which empties into the Atlantic via the Santa Cruz River.

The Lanín Volcano in Lanín National Park stands 12,400 feet (3,776 m) high. Its majestic figure, with its glacial peak, can be seen from far off on the steppe. Located between Lake Tromen to the north and Lake Paimún to the south, its southern side is shaped like a pyramid and dominates the landscape for miles. Every summer hikers climb this volcanic mountain in Northern Patagonia. From its peak, on clear days it is possible to make out the Pacific Ocean on the horizon, over an expansive landscape of mountains and volcanoes on the Chilean side of the region.

In the central part of western Santa Cruz, the lakes of Perito Moreno National Park dazzle with the rich turquoise hue of their waters. Tierra del Fuego has few lakes, but it is well worth visiting its largest, Lake Fagnano.

A myriad of crystalline rivers runs between the mountains, born from or emptying into the lakes. Many are ideal for fishing or adventure tourism. One example is the Futaleufú River in Chile, which is considered one of the world's most challenging sites for white-water kayaking.

The southwest is characterized by the majesty of its mountains, some of which figure among the earth's most impressive. The most important rise in the region of the Continental Ice Fields, both in Argentina and Chile. Their sharp, pointy peaks preside over fantastic landscapes that have challenged many of the world's best mountain climbers over the years.

The monkey puzzle tree (*Araucaria araucana*) is a magnificent species found exclusively in the province of Neuquén. Its shape is unmistakable, with a wide, full crown atop a trunk that can measure 150 feet (45 m) in height and 6 feet (2 m) in diameter. This species is most prevalent in cold and humid areas between 3,000 and 6,000 feet (900–1,800 m) above sea level. Its highly nutritious seeds are consumed by various animal species, and have always been an important food source for the region's aboriginal peoples.

Numerous volcanoes are another outstanding feature of the Andes; in Patagonia, especially in the north, these enormous conical hills, most of which are topped off with glacial caps, are sights well worth seeing.

The North and South Continental Ice Fields are gigantic glaciers separated by channels from the Chilean Sea. The central part of the glacial area and its branches are surrounded by mountains, many ice-covered.

The largest is the South Continental Ice Field, some 220 miles (350 km) in length and ranging between 30 and 50 miles (50 and 80 km) in width.

Off the main glacial plain, both eastwards and westwards, long river branches stretch out, ending in enormous lakes. In some cases on the western slope, they culminate in fjords and channels in the archipelagoes of southern Chile.

Several of these glacial branches are accessible to tourists. In fact, they have won international fame and each year attract more visitors. The principal ones are found in Los Glaciers National Park in the southwest of Santa Cruz, Argentina.

Another great glacier, although smaller than the Continental Ice Fields, is the Cordillera Darwin Ice Field on the southwest of Isla Grande. Several branches descend from it towards the Beagle Channel on the Chilean side.

The archipelagoes of southern Chile are also enchanting. The northern part spreads out in a north-south direction, from Isla Grande de Chile to the islands north of the Taitao Peninsula, along the final stretch of the Andes on the Chilean coast.

The fragmentation of the Andes into a great number of islands and areas divided by deep fjords and channels represents its most vast zone. The archipelagoes begin in the Gulf of Penas; at the western mouth of the Strait of Magellan they shift to a northwest-southeast course; and then they wind up at the Wollaston Islands, where Cape Horn emerges.

The great number of mountainous islands and extensive channels that make up this archipelago give a magical air to this not-so-accessible region boasting important national parks and reserves.

Besides affording one of the planet's most beautiful settings, the forests and the southern Andes reaffirm, with their diverse landscapes and fauna, the natural wealth of spectacular Patagonia.

The Circuito chico area *(above left)* of Nahuel Huapí National Park in Río Negro is visited by thousands of tourists each season. In the foreground is El Trébol Lagoon; behind it, Perito Moreno Lake; and in the background, Lake Nahuel Huapí, dominated by the towering Capilla Hill. The area is peppered by villages with magnificent summer homes and hotels, among which the traditional Hotel Llao-Llao *(above)* truly stands out. Opened in 1938, it is located on a site with breathtaking views of the gorgeous surrounding countryside between Lakes Nahuel Huapí and Perito Moreno.

Forests of cinnamon-barked trees (members of the myrtle family) grow in their natural state in very few places. They prefer humid sites, usually on the banks of rivers or lakes. In the northern area of Lake Nahuel Huapí in Neuquén, there is a wonderful forest of this species in Los Arrayanes National Park, which was created with the conservation of these trees in mind. The forest is a favorite stop for travelers making lake excursions from Villa La Angostura to the north and from Puerto Pañuelo in the Llao-Llao area on the Río Negro.

Mount Tronador, 11,411 feet (3,478 m) in height, is Nahuel Huapí National Park's most outstanding mountain, offering a spectacular landscape of large, rugged glaciers which, descending from its three summits, cover the better part of the mountain. Its name, which means "thundering," alludes to the frequent sounds of great blocks of ice breaking off the glacial masses. Hiking and mountain-climbing enthusiasts access Mount Tronador via a trail that leads to the Otto Meiling Refuge where they can lodge and explore the surroundings or take off for one of its summits.

The fantastic Blue River Valley, very close to the city of El Bolsón in Río Negro, extends south to Lake Puelo, Chubut. This entire area, shared by the two provinces, is a tranquil region with farms and houses spread in a geographic dreamland with a very pleasant microclimate. In this valley travelers find numerous natural attractions and a wide spectrum of outdoor activities, making their base at El Bolsón or staying at the camp sites near the river.

Los Alerces Glacier on the eastern side of Mount Tronador *(opposite page)*.

The Quemquemtreu River runs through the El Bolsón Valley, crossing the city's urban areas, to later join with the Azul River further south *(left page)*.

An important offshoot of the Azul River is the Blanco River, also called the Motoco River, which offers a magnificent landscape along its last stretch. This area is accessible by paths that run through a dense forest. Giant rocks in its riverbed create beautiful cascades and backwaters, the flow of which varies according to the season of the year, being most powerful at the beginning of the summer.

The Azul River finally empties into Lake Puelo in the national park of the same name in Chubut. Its turquoise waters make a vivid impression, set against a landscape dominated by Tres Picos Hill on the southern horizon. This is the most-visited lake in the region because of its easy accessibility. It also has a pleasant resort area.

Lake Cholila in Chubut is the first in a great system of lakes connected by rivers that carry their waters from the north to the south, to later turn westwards, cross the Andes and finally empty into the Pacific Ocean. Along with the Carrileufú River into which it drains, the Cholila is a renowned site for fly fishing.

The Menendez River in Los Alerces National Park in Chubut, which runs between Lakes Verde and Menendez, dazzles with the color of its crystalline waters.

The imposing Torrecillas Hill, with its great glaciers, provides one of the most beautiful views at Los Alerces National Park *(left page)*.

The lahuan forests, as the native people called the Patagonian cypress, are the object of conservation at Los Alerces National Park, created in 1937. This scarce tree species grows to great heights and diameters, some living thousands of years. The example in the photo at right measures 187 feet (57 m) in height; its base is 7 feet (2.20 m) in diameter; and it is 2,600 years old.

Lake Futalaufquen, in Los Alerces National Park, on a rainy day. The great beauty of the lake and mountain scenery in Patagonia is always awe-inspiring, regardless of the weather conditions; in fact, overcast afternoons on the shores of a southern lake can evoke a sense of great inner peace.

The city of Esquel, nestled in the valley of the same name, was founded in 1906. Its population was initially made up of Welsh immigrants who were later joined by others of different nationalities. It has always been an important supply center for the region, increasing its commercial activity in 1945 when the narrow-gauge railroad line reached Esquel. At the other end of the line, in Ingeniero Jacobacci, it linked with the national railroad network, which connected Esquel to Buenos Aires. Currently, the city is enjoying a growth in its tourism industry. Travelers use it as a base from which to visit Los Alerces National Park, La Hoya Winter Retreat, and other attractions in the area.

The Trevelin Regional Museum *(opposite)* is housed in a former wheat mill. Its collection contains many interesting pieces that illuminate the history of Welsh colonization of the area, which began in 1865.

One of the falls of the Natt and Fall Cascades in the western-central area of the 16th of October Valley, an area of transition between the southern woods and the steppe; the cordillera cypress woods grow here.

Following spread: A road winds through the landscape of farms in the 16th of October Valley. The fertility of its land and the presence of several rivers appropriate for irrigation made this region, from Esquel to the south, an ideal spot for Welsh immigrants to settle towards the end of the 19th century.

The Andean-Patagonian forest is the planet's southernmost woodland, which is why it is also referred to as sub-Antarctic. Trees carpet the sides of the mountains, stretching down to the shores of the lakes. While it is an extensive region in length, measuring some 1,366 miles (2,200 km), its average width in Argentina is 31 miles (50 km), with a maximum width of 47 miles (75 km).

While summer is the best season to enjoy the southern forest, autumn also presents very attractive possibilities. Especially at the beginning of fall, the forest takes on an appearance that overwhelms the observer with a wide range of intense colors that, like an artistic collage, create a surprising texture. Thus, the reds, oranges, ochers and yellows, splashed with some perennial greens, harmonize with the blues of the lakes, offering one of the most sublime visual poems on Earth. The first snowfalls arrive in autumn, and the interior of the snow-covered forest astounds the senses with its silence and luminosity *(following pages)*.

The flowers of the forest adorn the woodlands with their intense colors, contrasting beautifully with the predominant greens. Pictured are aljaba *(left)*; amancay *(top)*; notro *(above)*.

Many water courses descend from the mountains, produced by rain or the melting of snow or ice at their highest points. Known as *chorriyos*, these constantly flowing streams cross the interior of the forest, stimulating the growth of minor vegetation species that require a lot of humidity. These species carpet the forest's borders, where a variety of interesting amphibians dwell.

The so-called Valdivian jungle, primarily occupying the Chilean side of the region, represents the most humid environment of the Andean-Patagonian forest. Its relatively stable temperatures and rainfall, which exceeds 150 inches (400 cm) annually in some areas, allow for the growth of a diverse and plentiful vegetation made up of ferns, epiphytes and vines, among other species. The very common *coligüe* (a leafy creeper) forms dense and impenetrable thickets. The environment's great humidity and profuse vegetation give it the appearance of a tropical jungle. It is in this environment that the Patagonian cypress grows, towering over the luxuriant undergrowth.

Los Glaciares National Park, in southwestern Santa Cruz (Argentina) is an internationally renowned natural attraction, and was declared a World Heritage Site by UNESCO in 1981. Each year it is visited by thousands of tourists from Argentina and elsewhere attracted by the formidable Perito Moreno Glacier. The glacier's face measures 14,765 feet (4,500 m) in length and it rises 195 feet (60 m) above the water. It is strategically located in a valley between great mountains opposite the enormous Magallanes Peninsula on Lake Argentino, which offers the perfect vantage point for observing the glacier's back region. The frequent sight and sound of enormous ice chunks breaking off and crashing into the water provides a memorable experience for visitors. After advancing until it is pressed against the peninsula's edge like a dike, the glacier's face sometimes collapses under the pressure and force of the backed-up waters of the Rico Arm of Lake Argentino, creating a particularly spectacular crash into the sea.

Flooded coastal area of the Rico arm of Lake Argentino, inundated by the water dammed up by the Moreno Glacier. The dead trees along the shoreline are casualties of the flooding *(left page)*.

The Upsala Glacier is the largest arm of the South Patagonian Continental Ice Field. It is 30 miles (50 km) long; its face is 6 miles (10 km) wide; and it towers 320 feet (100 m) above the northernmost sector of Lake Argentino.

A gigantic iceberg that has broken off from the face of the Upsala Glacier. These massive chunks of ice slowly drift along the lake and take a great deal of time to melt completely *(previous spread)*.

The Viedma Glacier, on the lake of the same name, is the northernmost of the branches that descend off the South Continental Ice Field onto great bodies of water in Los Glaciares National Park *(left page)*.

The principal plain of the South Continental Ice Field is found in Bernardo O'Higgins National Park in Chile. It measures 220 miles (354 km) in length, and its width varies between 30 and 50 miles (50-80 km). In the foreground, Gorra Blanca Range; on the horizon, Lautaro Volcano.

The extreme north of Los Glaciares National Park is dominated by an imposing group of granitic mountains, featuring the Fitz Roy Range and the Torre Range. Their summits, which are celebrated in the world of mountain climbing, tower more than 9,000 feet (3,000 m) above sea level. Aggressively jutting up from the earth, they can be seen from several miles away. Mount Fitz Roy was called Chaltén by the aboriginal population, who believed it to be a volcano. Accompanied by the spiraling Poincenot and other adjacent peaks, it is one of the most well-known images of Patagonia. Mount Torre, with its impressive slopes and permanently snow-capped summit, has always represented an especially difficult challenge even for world-class mountain climbers due to its violent and unpredictable climate.

The settlement of El Chaltén at the foot of the Fitz Roy Range was founded in the early 1980s. Currently it is booming with an important expansion in its tourist services. It is the base camp for climbing expeditions and excursions to the South Continental Ice Field. Each summer it overflows with hiking, mountain-climbing and nature enthusiasts who come to take advantage of the region's great range of outdoor activities.

Southwestern Santa Cruz has always dazzled travelers with its cloud formations, which frequently assume surprising shapes and configurations, set against intensely blue skies and harmonizing majestically with the lakes *(left page)*.

Flocks of flamingos occasionally adorn the most tranquil coastal areas of the lakes at the foot of the south Andes.

The city of Ushuaia, on the shores of the Beagle Channel, on Tierra del Fuego's Isla Grande. Its name means "bay that enters to the west" in the language of the Yahgan Indians, the original inhabitants of the region, along with other aboriginal cultures. Located at the foot of the Martial Mountains, dominated in the northeast by the magnificent Mount Olivia, it is Tierra del Fuego's tourist base. It is also the closest sea and air port to Antarctica.

Les Eclaireurs Lighthouse on one of the islands of the Beagle Channel, opposite Ushuaia.

An imperial shag colony on Isla Alice. The group of rocky islands near the mouth of Ushuaia Bay are inhabited by a great number of birds and sea lions. It is a favorite stop on boat excursions through the Beagle Channel.

A glacier descending on the Beagle Channel, stemming from the Cordillera Darwin Ice Field in Alberto De Agostini National Park in the Chilean region of Tierra del Fuego, west of Ushuaia.

The Harberton Estancia, on the east coast of the Beagle Channel, was established in 1886 by the Reverend Thomas Bridges, the first white man to settle in Tierra del Fuego. The stunning natural scenery in which it is set, as well as its historical importance, have made it a popular stop for tourists arriving both by land and by boat.

A stunning southern sunset over the Beagle Channel *(following spread)*.

In autumn, lengas (a member of the southern beech family) are furiously set ablaze, magically reaffirming the name Tierra del Fuego ("Land of Fire") *(left page)*.

A stretch of the Pipo River in Tierra del Fuego National Park.

In the south of Isla Grande, in Tierra del Fuego, there are valleys with wide-open areas in which solid ground alternates with peat bogs, flooded lowlands in which dead vegetation does not decompose due to the great acidity of the water. It continually accumulates, forming multiple layers, one over the other *(right page)*.

The Lapataia River, in Tierra del Fuego National Park, carries the waters of Lake Roca to the Beagle Channel, crossing the beautiful countryside dominated by Mount Cóndor.

Typical rural wooden houses in the south of Chile with their upright roofing tiles, the most commonly used for modest buildings.
On the horizon, the Osorno Volcano with its icy summit, 8,700 feet (2,652 m) in height *(right page)*.

Lake Escondido, in the south of Tierra del Fuego, seen from the Luis Garibaldi Pass. In this area, the Andes run west to east,
and it is through this pass that National Route 3 crosses from the north to the south.

The Lake of All Saints is an important attraction within the Vicente Pérez Rosales National Park in Region X in Chile. Its mirror-like waters reflect the beauty of the eastern side of the Osorno Volcano.

Lake Puelo in Chubut, Argentina, drains westward through the Puelo River into Lower Lake Puelo *(following spread)*, which lies in Chile's Region X. The lower lake in turn drains into Reloncavi Sound via the Lower Puelo River.

The locals regularly cross the fierce waters of the Puelo River by boat to reach their homes. Many of these areas lack roads, so transportation takes place on foot, on horseback, or by boat. This river heads west from Lake Puelo in Argentina, carrying its waters to the Chilean sea *(above left)*.

Colorful fishing boats adorn the harbor scenery of the city of Puerto Montt, on the shores of the Reloncavi Sound. The waters of this coastal area in the south of Chile are particularly rich in fish, the traditional food source for the local population *(above)*.

The distinctive architecture of the south of Chile, in this case Isla de Chilóe, is a renowned attraction appreciated by travelers from around the world *(left)*.

The massive Torres del Paine mountains, with their sheer, vertical walls, dominate the scenery in the national park of the same name.

Torres del Paine is Chile's most spectacular national park. It is located south of the South Continental Ice Field, several glacial arms of which stretch into the park. The magnificence of its scenery is characterized by its great mountains and its beautiful lakes, such as Lake Pehoé, and the imposing group of hills dominated by the summits of the Cuernos del Paine *(pages 141 and 142).*

The Paine Massif, seen from the pre-Andean steppe, where crystalline lagoons abound.

Water courses descending from mountain glaciers often become turbulent due to the precipitous drops in the region's landscape.

The city of Puerto Natales *(right page)*, on the shores of the Almirante Montt Gulf in the north of the Magallanes Region, is the base for exploring Torres del Paine National Park, offering an attractive array of services that expands as Patagonia becomes an increasingly popular tourist destination.

Tourism
in Patagonia

Thanks to its dazzling and pristine natural environment, Patagonia is among the world's most spectacular tourist destinations. Currently, it is one of the regions most visited by tourists from all over the planet, and its popularity grows each year.

The region offers the visitor a variety of activities and destinations, regardless of the season. Traveling on your own or with a planned tour, you will discover awe-inspiring landscapes and wildlife of unexpected beauty as you cross this vast territory. Your visit to Patagonia is sure to leave a profound emotional mark on you.

Traveling by land from north to south, eastern Patagonia is accessed from Buenos Aires via National Route 3. From the Province of La Pampa, various highways run through central Patagonia.

Whale-watching near Puerto Pirámide on the Valdés Peninsula, Chubut, Argentina.

Western Patagonia can be reached from Mendoza via National Route 40, Argentina's longest highway, which runs through the western part of the country from Jujuy to the city of Río Gallegos in Santa Cruz.

Patagonia can also be reached by air; there are airports in the most important cities.

On the Chilean side of the region, the Pan-American Highway is the major land route, and the airports of the principal cities offer air access as well.

The many highways and secondary roads crisscrossing the region's interior provide access to the principal tourist attractions. The roads unite points both in Argentina and Chile, making it possible to combine areas of both countries in your itinerary by using the mountain passes.

The Eastern Zone

Southern Buenos Aires and Río Negro

Patagonia's Atlantic region represents Argentina's most extensive coastal zone, and it boasts various areas of interest to tourists.

In the extreme south of the province of Buenos Aires, Anegada Bay and San Blas Bay stand out as excellent options for fishing enthusiasts.

There are some seaside resorts in the province of Río Negro, such as Las Grutas, to the south of San Antonio Oeste, with the warmest waters of Patagonia.

On the province's northern shores, the Punta Bermeja Sea Lion Colony Reserve is situated, the first of its kind on the Patagonian coast.

Chubut

Crossing the 42nd parallel, one enters the province of Chubut, home to the Valdés Peninsula, an internationally acclaimed wildlife reserve and one of the most popular tourist destinations in South America.

This peninsula, with its stunningly steep and rocky coastline and its blue waters, is the place chosen by a diverse range of marine animals to make their homes; southern right whales and southern elephant seals are but a few of the species to be seen here. The most popular attraction consists of a network of wildlife reserves that are easy to get to by the peninsula's roads.

Puerto Pirámide is the only village on the Valdés Peninsula. It is a picturesque spot to spend the night. Whale watching excursions take off from here as well. Its sandy white beaches transform this village into a lovely seaside resort in the summertime.

On the Nuevo Gulf, south of the Valdés Peninsula, sits the city of Puerto Madryn, the scuba diving capital. Its waters offer excellent opportunities to observe underwater landscapes and their fauna. Sea lions and dolphins, driven by their natural curiosity, will frequently approach divers.

In summer, the sprawling beaches of this city and its surroundings are transformed into one of Patagonia's principal seaside resort areas. Each season the local residents welcome visitors from all over the country, and they are rightly famous for being the perfect hosts.

Puerto Madryn is Patagonia's most important port, home to a thriving fishing industry. It is also a port of call for cruise ships heading for the Valdés Peninsula and Punta Tombo.

Some miles to the south of the city, the Punta Loma Wildlife Reserve is found. It is a sea lion rookery not far from Cerro Avanzado.

Puerto Pirámide, on the Valdés Peninsula, is located in the most beautiful and sheltered area of the Nuevo Gulf in Chubut, Argentina.

Continuing south, the Lower Valley of the Chubut River makes for an attractive setting for the cities of Trelew, Gaiman, Rawson (the capital of Chubut), and the seaside resort of Playa Unión. The valley's network of roads carries the traveler through wooded landscapes crossed by the Chubut River, on whose banks the legacy of Welsh colonization can be appreciated, including the typical chapels and houses in Gaiman and Dolavon.

Seventy-five miles (120 km) southwest of Trelew stands the Florentino Ameghino Dam along with its little town located in an awesome rocky canyon through which the Chubut River runs.

From Trelew you can easily get to the Punta Tombo Wildlife Reserve, home to the principal Magellanic penguin breeding colony. There you can walk among thousands of penguins scurrying back and forth to the sea, busily building their nests.

In the south of the province, the city of Comodoro Rivadavia is the gateway to the southern coast of Patagonia. To the west, the

The city of Puerto Madryn in Chubut, Argentina.

remains of trees that millions of years ago stood up to 300 feet (100 m) high can be admired at the José Ormachea Petrified Forest Geological Reserve.

Santa Cruz

In the northeast of Santa Cruz, Puerto Deseado and Cape Blanco have cornered the tourism market, thanks to their rugged rock formations and their rich animal life.

The Deseado estuary offers the traveler excursions on water and strolls along its shores, and Cape Blanco boasts the most beautiful lighthouse on the Argentine coast.

To the west of Puerto Deseado, towards the interior of the province, the Petrified Forest Natural Monument is easy to get to via National Route 3.

The Western Zone

Neuquén

In the province of Neuquén, the Lanín National Park, with San Martin de Los Andes as its base, stands out along with the Seven Lakes circuit. Another possible tourist route is to cross into Chile by way of three different mountain passes: Mamuil Malal, Carirriñe and Hua Hum.

The Huechulafquen, Paimún, Tomen, Lolog and Lacar Lakes are outstanding features of Lanín National Park, all forming part of breathtaking wooded landscapes framed by enormous mountains, dominated by the Lanín Volcano.

The Chimehuín River, which begins at the eastern outlet of Lake Huechulafquen, is a well-known spot for fly fishing and attracts anglers from around the world.

San Martin de Los Andes and its surroundings represent one of the most stunning areas in western Patagonia. It is linked to Chile by the Hua Hum Pass, and offers multiple recreational activities.

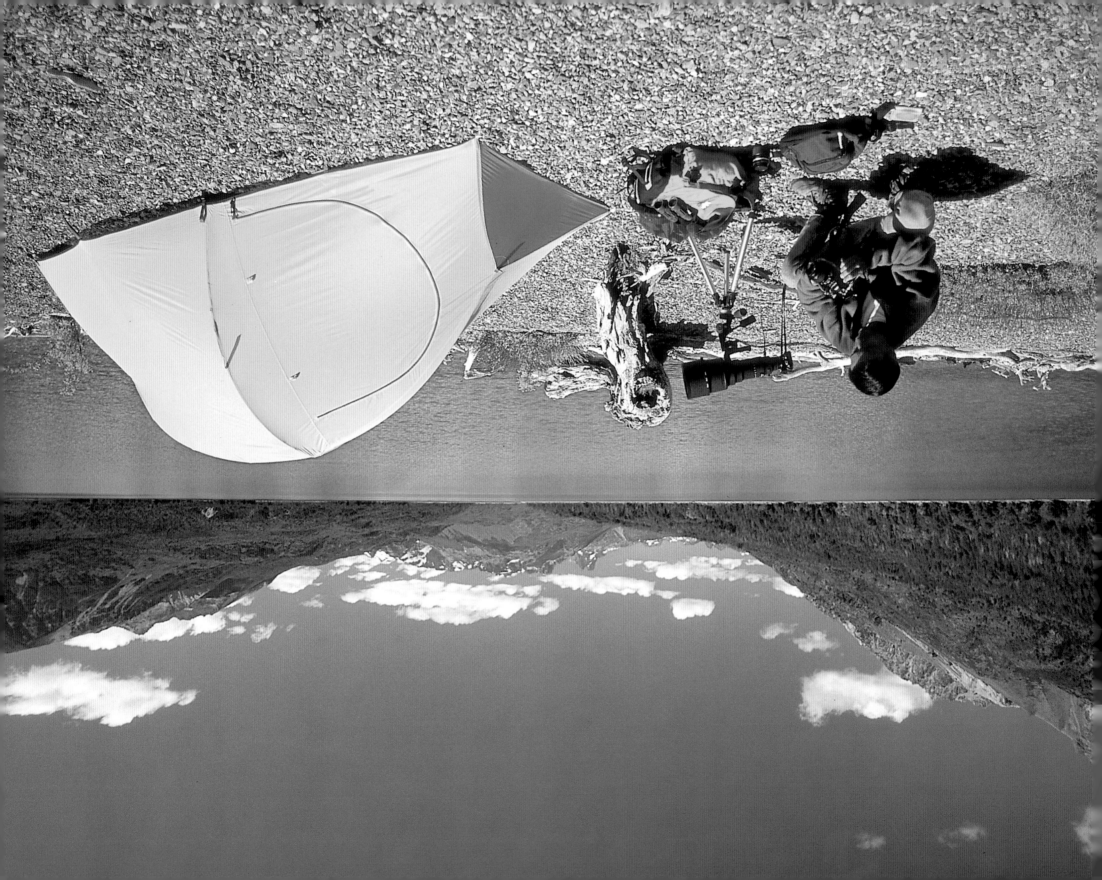

In winter, the Chapelco ski resort is known for its excellent network of runs and facilities.

Heading south, Nahuel Huapí National Park is reached following the Seven Lakes circuit. Along the way, landscapes of forests and mountains delight the eye, while stopovers can be made at towns like Villa La Angostura, the Cerro Bayo ski resort, and Los Arrayanes National Park. From the Villa La Angostura area it is possible to cross into Chile via the Cardenal A. Samoré Pass to visit Puyehue National Park.

Río Negro

San Carlos de Bariloche borders on Nahuel Huapí National Park. This city, along with Llao-Llao and the Cerro Catedral ski resort, make up the most popular tourist area in the Argentine Andes, accessible both by land and by air.

In summer, there are numerous recreational options: hikes along the trails that link various mountain retreats; excursions on Lake Nahuel Huapí and its river branches; and strolls along the banks of the region's numerous lakes and rivers.

In winter, Cerro Catedral comes alive. Argentina's most traditional ski resort, Cerro Catedral is not far from Bariloche and always draws large crowds of winter-sport enthusiasts.

From the Llao-Llao area, it is possible to enter Chile by boat through organized tours along the Blest branch of Lake Nahuel Huapí. Then, crossing the Vicente Pérez Rosales Pass, you arrive at the Chilean city of Puerto Montt.

To the south of Bariloche, the great El Bolsón Valley stretches out, boasting the most gorgeous countryside in the western Andes as well as a pleasant climate. It is home to the city of El Bolsón and is surrounded by attractive scenery, such as the Azul River Valley and the Piltriquitrón Hill.

Chubut

Some miles further south, in the province of Chubut, lie the towns of Hoyo de Epuyén and Lago Puelo, nestled in fertile valleys and quite near Lago Puelo National Park, with its stunning lake of the same name.

This valley region along the 42nd parallel in Río Negro and Chubut is ideal for outdoor activities such as hiking, horseback riding, river boating, camping and fishing.

The sweets made from this valley's fruits, as well as many other homemade products, are famous and are exhibited in the region's annual fairs and festivals.

Northwestern Chubut has numerous lakes and rivers. Los Alerces National Park contains awe-inspiring bodies of water, many interconnected by rivers, all forming the largest Andean lake basin. It begins north of the park at Lake Cholila and ends in Chile with the Futaleufú River as it empties into Lake Yelcho.

At Los Alerces National Park it is possible to take part in marvelous lake excursions and explore the woodlands where remarkable Patagonian cypress forests are protected. This is one of the southern zone's most famous tree species. The park's lake area is also wonderful for fishing, hiking and horseback riding.

Not far from Los Alerces National Park we find the city of Esquel, the base of the tourist circuit in northwestern Chubut. It has numerous attractions both in summer and in winter, a favorite of the latter season being the La Hoya ski resort.

From Esquel, passing through the town of Trevelin, one can cross into Chile via the Futaleufú Pass. Further on, the southern highway invites you through one of Chile's most beautiful regions.

Santa Cruz

In the central west of Santa Cruz, we find Perito Moreno National Park, an area of spectacular lakes and landscapes. It can be reached both from the north and the south via National Route 40. It is ideal for hiking, and with any luck you might catch sight of an Andean deer, one of the world's rarest deer species, unique to the Patagonian Andes.

North of the park a spot dominated by Mount San Lorenzo is a favorite among hiking and mountain-climbing enthusiasts.

In southwestern Santa Cruz, Los Glaciares National Park commands respect as one of the world's most spectacular protected areas. Its glaciers stemming off the South Patagonian Continental Ice Field represent an incomparable attraction.

The massive Upsala Glacier can be visited only by launch. The most famous, the Perito Moreno Glacier, has a structure that allows for walks over the ice of one of its sectors. It is accessible by land from the city of El Calafate, the region's tourist base.

In the park's northern zone, a settlement called El Chaltén is found at the foot of a mountain system formed by the Fitz Roy and Torre ranges. A Mecca for mountain climbers and hikers, it is also the base from which expeditions to the South Patagonian Continental Ice Field take off.

The Southern Zone

Tierra del Fuego
The city of Ushuaia, on the shores of the Beagle Channel, is the region's tourist center. Situated near the Tierra del Fuego National Park, it is the principal port of departure for cruises and flights to Antarctica.

Tierra del Fuego offers a wide spectrum of activities: excursions through the Beagle Channel or the national park; visits to traditional estancias; and hiking and horseback riding. In winter, one can enjoy skiing, snowmobiling and sleigh riding. The latter has become very popular in Tierra del Fuego over the last decade, given the area's excellent snowfall.

Also worth mentioning is the superior salmon fishing on the rivers and lakes. The base for this activity is the city of Río Grande, in the northern zone of Tierra del Fuego.

Chile

Region XII
From Tierra del Fuego one can head west to Chile's Region XII crossing the Strait of Magellan towards the city of Punta Arenas, and from there accessing the southern zone of the Magallanes region.

Traveling north on National Route 9, the city of Puerto Natales appears, the tourist base for the Última Esperanza zone in the north of the Magallanes region.

Several excursions leave from Puerto Natales, offering different exploration options, such as launches to glaciers and trips through the southern archipelagoes down to Puerto Montt.

Just a few miles from this city sits the Milodun Cavern Natural Monument, with a depth of 650 feet (200 m) and a height of 100 feet (30 m).

Continuing north, we find one of the world's most spectacular protected areas. Torres del Paine National Park features a system of lakes and rivers of great beauty with imposing mountains, such as the Torres and the Cuernos del Paine, both prime destinations for world-class mountain climbers.

The city of Ushuaia, Tierra del Fuego, Argentina.

Perito Moreno Glacier, Los Glaciares National Park, Santa Cruz, Argentina.
(following pages)

An ample network of trails allows hikers to cover a great part of the park, and a launch excursion brings visitors up to the Grey Glacier. .

Through the Cancha Carrera Pass it is possible to cross back into Argentina and head to El Calafate and Los Glaciares National Park. You can also get to Argentina from Puerto Natales traveling east towards Río Gallegos.

Regions XI and X

Heading north, Chile's Region XI watches over both the North Patagonian Continental Ice Field and the San Valentin Ice Field. From there it extends westward to the San Rafael Glacier in Laguna San Rafael National Park, a popular tourist attraction in southern Chile that can be reached by boat from Puerto Montt.

The southern highway that covers the south of Chile begins in Puerto Montt and leads visitors to picturesque towns like

Riding excursions are an attractive way to explore the natural landscapes of Patagonia.

Hornopirén, Chaitén, Puerto Cisnes, Puerto Aisen, Coihaique and Cochrane. There are numerous points of interest on this circuit, such as the Alerce Andino, Hornopirén and Queulat National Parks. In several areas it is possible to combine land travel with water excursions through channels and islands.

The General Carrera Lake stands out along the highway's southern zone. An alternative is to cross over to Argentina from Chile Chico to Los Antiguos, and then head east or south.

Isla Grande de Chilóe, with its numerous minor islands, is found in Region X. The architecture of this region warrants special attention, with its homes lined with stunning tiles and hundreds of old churches and chapels. Another attraction is the great diversity of arts and crafts made by its inhabitants, whose way of life is intimately tied to the land and the sea.

The North of Regions X and IX

To the north, now firmly on continental territory, Regions X and IX astound the eye with a series of great lakes set against the backdrop of a long chain of volcanoes.

The most important cities are Puerto Montt, on the shores of the Reloncaví Sound, which is the point of departure for boat excursions through channels and islands; Puerto Varas, on Lake Llanquihue; Osorno; Valdivia; and Temuco.

Not to be missed are the Alerce Andino, Vicente Pérez Rosales, Puyehue, Villarrica, Huerquehue, Conguillio Los Paraguas and Nahuelbuta National Parks; the Antillanca (in Puyehue) and Villarrica ski centers; and a great number of natural hot springs.

Both regions are crossed by the Southern Pan-American Highway, which branches off into hundreds of secondary roads leading to places of interest. Several mountain passes link these regions to tourist zones in the Argentine provinces of Río Negro and Neuquén.

De Agostini Glacier, Tierra del Fuego, Chile.

Photo Credits

Axel Bos: pages 14, 16, 18, 33, 34, 36, 37, 38-39, 40, 41, 42, 43, 44, 45, 46, 47, 50, 51, 52, 53, 54, 55, 56-57, 68, 80, 81, 85.

Daniel Rivademar: pages 4-5, 8-9, 11, 19, 20-21, 22, 23, 24, 25, 26, 27, 28, 29, 30-31, 32, 35, 40 upper left, upper right, 41 upper left, lower right, 43 right, 48, 49, 58, 60, 61, 62, 64, 65, 66, 67, 69, 70, 71, 72, 73, 74, 75, 76, 77, 78-79, 82, 84, 86, 88, 89, 90, 91, 92, 93, 94, 95, 96, 97, 98, 99, 100, 101, 102-103, 104, 105, 106, 107, 108, 109, 110, 111, 112-113, 114, 115, 116, 117, 118, 119, 120, 121, 122, 123, 124, 125, 126, 127, 128, 129, 130, 131, 132, 133, 134, 135, 136-137, 138-139, 140, 141, 142, 143, 144, 145, 146, 147, 148, 149, 150, 151, 153, 154, 155, 156-157, 158, 159.

Published May 1999